My Chronic Battle with Loneliness

Tenets from being youthful and vigorously attempting to attain wisdom

Sukant Mukherjee

BookLeaf Publishing
India | USA | UK

Made with ❤ on the BookLeaf Publishing Platform
www.bookleafpub.in
www.bookleafpub.com

Dedication

This anthology is about all the hardships, betrayals and indifferences.

They ensured that the pillars that had to fall have disappeared, and the ones that were true stand taller and stronger than ever.

Each of them knows who I am referring to. Calling them out here would allow me to repay some of the gratitude, but I do not want to part with that enormous weight.

Instead, I will continue to strive to be useful to them.

Acknowledgement

To acknowledge is similar to apologising. If you truly regret something, you wouldn't just say "sorry", but you should accept the mistake and ensure that it wouldn't become your legacy. Similarly, a mere "thanks" defeats the purpose of recognising someone's contribution in making you, you. Instead it should be a part of your legacy.

With the above thought, I can't think of a greater disservice to individually call out the contributors. My words always tend to fail at the best (and worst) of times. They know who they are, and if they don't, then it is I who needs to ensure that it is beyond a reasonable doubt in their minds. That being said, I would like to thank God, the supposedly undead one.

That segues into the final segment of this page. I feel it is important for souls to have some form of companionship, and the ones who aren't as fortuitous to have been blessed with a support system or pillars. They can take solace in knowing there are predominantly dead people who don't discriminate while they are inviting you to their worlds.

These are the ones I was adopted by over the years:

Jim Morison
Friedrich Nietzsche
Franz Kafka
Guru Dutt
Kurt Cobain
Stanley Kubrick
Nick Drake
The Shaman

Foreword

I know what I'm saying, I don't know what you are hearing.
I know what I'm writing, I don't know what you are reading.
I know what I'm displaying, I don't know what you are seeing.

Because the sender and receiver might not be in the same realms shouldn't mean one is better than the other.
Goes without saying, all art is perception. But what you are perceiving doesn't mean that is being portrayed.
If you get triggered, it doesn't mean the artist had the intention to trigger.
If you are pleased, it doesn't mean the artist wanted to please!
A primordial aspect to remember is, if it doesn't appeal to you, close this and move on to the next. Do not dwell on anything that invokes indifference. But if it invokes emotion on either the positive or negative spectrums, then it is important to know the "why". Not just celebrate or castigate.

All of these might seem disjointed, and it may be so. The underlying theme here is to call out that nothing henceforth in this book should be considered to be a fact or an absolute, the words can be interpreted and misinterpreted according to your liking, same goes with the illustrations. The rest is entirely upon you.
But who am I to say anything about how you want to experience any of it? Do what you must. The only request is to keep the author out of it.

Preface

You understand me not, my words are not for everyone's eyes
I write my lyrics for them who still have ears to hear the unheard.
The only one who has fulfilled this is the reflection I see in the mirror
one must embrace mayhem to give birth to a supernova
what I say next is not just a prologue.
consider it as a caution, a warning, a deterrent.

Outside the dream, insidious insufficient
coagulated stones of showy preciousness
surround the soles of your feet.
Why is that never enough?
Will you ever feel the warmth in this wandering winter?
The tyrannical cloud of darkness is now your nimbus. You can either ride it, or perish in it.

Index

The Shaman's Ode to his Readers

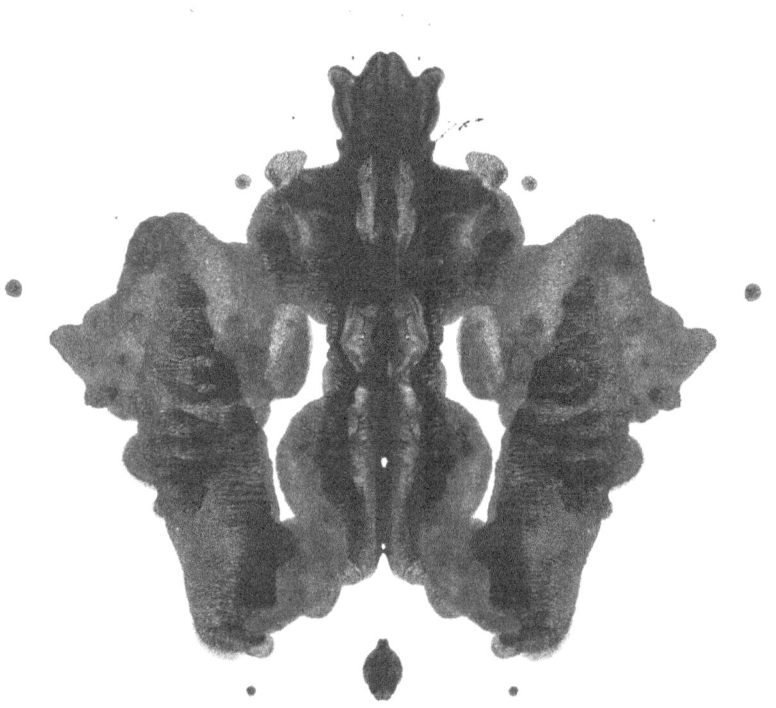

You! You die with no life, your life has no soul!
Your soul was an abysmal joke, you died, but I didn't take your life.
Kill me? All can do so.
Take my life? Let's see you try!
My soul is entirely mine—HA! WHO THERE SIGHED?
You say no one took your life?
Yet, you squirm when sinners enjoy their pleasure!
I shall now fulfil my desire.
But before I do, here is an ode—ode to all the scum embodied in your soul.
An ode to all the filth that you have incorporated amongst you.

Sick is not a state of mind,
Sick is not a state of mine.
Call me psychopath, 'tis a better term?
Well then, Psycho could be my little firm!
I'll cut your face,
I'll eat those eyes,

I'll drink its blood,
And you fools still don't know why!
Yes, I am a sinner,
But certainly not a killer.
At least I played for me.
What made you cry?
I behaved with guile,
I acted with style,
I walked on my own mile,
Tell me what made you eat your own bile?

You!!!!
You die with fear!
You die like a liar!
You die with tears!
You were all dead before your death!
It was a shame.
Shameful that you did not fight.

You robbed yourself the pleasure of life.
Worshipping the thieves of your living live.
Murderer, they called me. They could not be more vile!
Saviour, you called me. I hope that all of you are burnt in a massive pile.

Was I not sinister in my skill?
I did lack the hunger to pick up the quill.
All I did was fulfil my will.

Did I crush for fun to slay?
I didn't! Does that make you any less gay?
I am not the creep you think of me.
But you continue to be the creep I know of you!

Now it's time,
Time to embark on this new act.
Redemption is not what I deserve,
So my existence is something I should not preserve!

Fade Away

In the carnivorous carnival of my mind...
An overabundance of games are played.
I want to conquer the game, but I am unable to decide the prize...
Where is my spirit guide? Oh! that I have slayed.
What does my heart want? To not prepare for my demise.
It's time for me to desensitise...
Eternal damnation? Is this the new surprise?

Talking to you lifted me from my grave,
Clutching your hands forced me out of my cave...
I levitated off the ground when you bestowed your head ...
Yet the sky is not closer... is that something to dread?
Onset of limbo?
Where do I belong?
Is it time to fly from my window?
Is this my swan song?
What do I want? You!
What do I really want? I wish I knew...

Realisation struck!
Eyes numb, in those moments I am stuck!
Your laugh... my achievement!
Your smile... my bliss!
Your voice... my peace!
Your presence... my solace!
Break the illusion, rid myself of the hope!

Respect your call...
In line, I shall fall
Reluctantly, I crawl
Always, you above all.

Don't look at me... (it's time for me to leave)
My feet are unwilling to move... (I am set to depart)
My destiny awaits... (there is the exit)
I want to scream... (I do not want to go)

Ready to go... (stop me)
I am going... (stop me)
I am going... (stop me)
I am going... (stop me)
I am gone.
Apologies for not leaving sooner...

The Anti-Suicide Prose

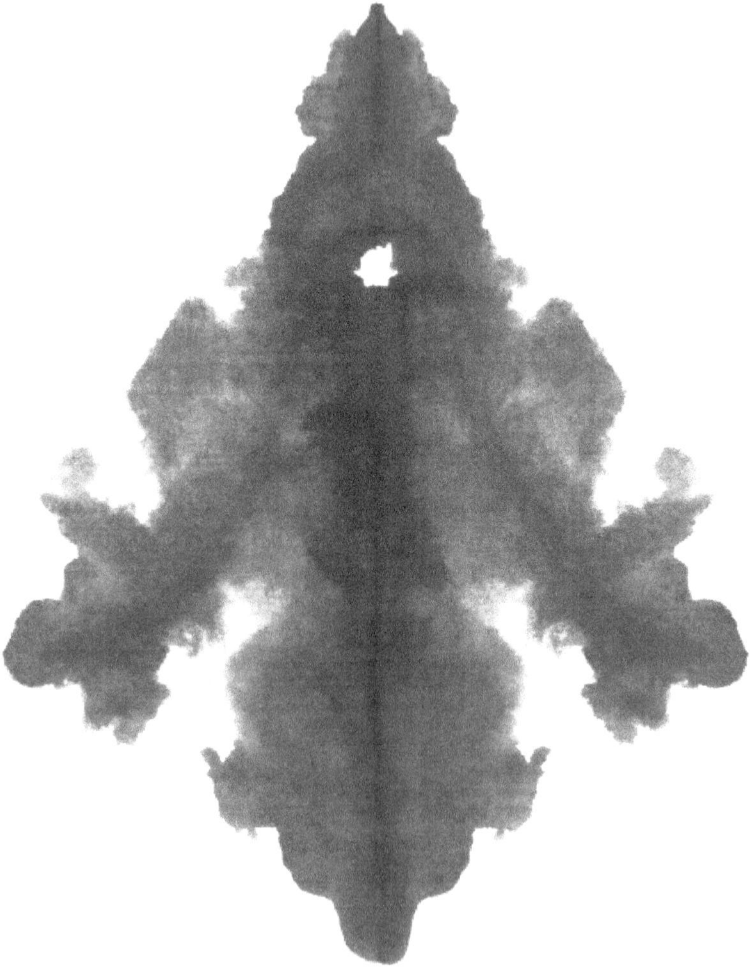

There is no greater sin
Than not raising your beaten chin
Especially when there is no calling from within
So, do not go... do not go gently into the void's darkest bin

No amount of hate
Nothing should lead you beyond the gate
Do not think ugly of your faceless fate
Do not go... do not go gently away from your mate

Sing! Sing! Sing along
Sing the song of greatest fears
Sing the songs of crippling heartbreaks
Sing the song of tyrannical pains
But do not mumble... do not mumble the words that draws the noose of the abyss

Ask yourself, your only self
What makes you jump, jump away, away from one-ness...
Why perform this great self-defacing sacrifice?

You will not be rewarded the drink from the goblet of god's own orifice
So let's all join—join this ballad of what we call life, and

Sing! Sing! Sing along
Sing the song of greatest fears
Sing the songs of crippling heartbreaks
Sing the song of tyrannical pains
but do not mumble, mumble the words that draws the noose of the abyss

Funeral Pyre

A barrel of a gun
A barrel from a ship
A farewell to the crib
Oh! How I wonder, when is my trip?

Do not flip, do not trick
Use the clip, use the brick
Ride the slip, don't get sick
This is not a rhyme! Is this my trip?

Dawned upon me what shouldn't have
I believed it to be true even though it couldn't have
Not the realisation of a new truth
But the revelation that I was worthy to realise that maybe, in actuality, I am not a brute.

In all this pandemonium on the outside of my inside world
The air of calmness has destroyed the jostle of much-needed psalm-ness
Oh, I pray to thee!! Help me destroy my evil twins
Kill them both, annihilate their souls
Why must both yin and yang reside within?

Why must I bare the burden of two?
Don't get me wrong, I wish the bliss for you too!
Take it away, let me give it away!
I am not worthy, I am not strong
Stop hiding your might in plain sight.

I didn't choose you, you aren't my choice!
Slacking like a sloth, you un-drapeable cloth!
I gave you the voice of a lion, yet you prowl like a scion of froth
Be gone from my sight! Worthless child of not
Rid you yourself this life, let your soul die and rot
Though I am your creator, do not hover like a moth
There is no light for you
There is no redemption for you
There is no salvation for you
There is no existence for you
Nothing will precede you
Nothing will succeed you
You are all but a vessel enforced upon me
All because you acted righteously
Undo your sin of not committing any

End the turmoil of this eternal reconnoitring
You cannot wield the power of this gift
You cannot spread the joy of this gift
Bring to end my bitterness
Gallantry is not accustomed to weaknesses
But knowing you, I have overstepped my
bounds, rekindling your fire
Let me assure you this test is not a test, but
rather your funeral pyre!

In Morbidity, I Thrive

I start this piece with my patented
disclaimers:
In morbidity, I thrive.
In agony, I effortlessly drive.
Easier to wallow in pain.
Loneliness is my only friend in the rain.
I trust that in happiness, I have nothing to
gain.

Falling for you gave me so much pleasure
The reason for this pleasure stemmed from
displeasure
Every time you rejected me, it made me feel
lesser
An affirmation to my belief: life is nothing
but a depressor.

In the kiss, there was despair
Beyond repair, when you shrugged it off as a
measly affair
Kept gasping for air in this self-inflicted
psychological warfare
Conniving myself to care, when all you did
was be unaware

This nightmare is not something anyone wants to bear.

Scary was the intimacy, because it caused unparalleled ecstasy
Frightened of being apart, terrified more of not being able to let go
Afraid of showing my feelings, petrified of seeing yours
The happiness of your presence has made me unconsciously want to face my fears.

A stereotype but true nevertheless,
You brought colour into my life.
Without you, I felt like I was in a black bland abyss.

When your affection grew stronger,
The excuse I gave? Distance made the heart grow fonder.
You missed me, that it affirmed all your doubts
I longed for you, that it made me miserable.

It was easy for me to believe that I could be
your happiness
It was unbearable for me to even ponder that
you are the reason for mine.

I was convinced that I needed to disengage,
before eventually you would separate
Craftily becoming a prisoner in a cage,
someone you would ultimately hate.

With fastidious faith, I believed that the joy
you brought would only reign in agony
Yet, in this, I felt a noble glory.

Then you uttered those three magnificent
words
I cajoled myself that your vision is
impaired.Having you back in my arms felt
like home
Yet, I was sure someday you'd be gone.
When you said you were in love,
I was assured that it was all a hoax, a cruel
joke!

Every time you showed affection

In time I knew it'd transform into dejection.

Time, I thought, moved linearly
But suddenly it jumped exponentially.
It brought you unprecedented sorrow.
Excellent for me, I flourish in misery.
Being your rock came naturally.
I felt splendour in being a boatman to
navigate through your despondency.

Then came "the night"
Suddenly there was the establishment of an
unbreakable connection!
A bond of the soul
An unfaltering link
An association for life
The intertwining of two lives into one.
Euphoria! Exultation! Ecstasy! Elation!
Jubilation! Bliss...
Just being with you made me feel like I was in
paradise.
There grew a sudden resentment towards the
cherished indispositions
A revulsion towards my treasured possessions

A hostile distaste started to grow towards this abhorrence.

I no longer have an excuse as to why you care
I no longer have reasons to believe that this is a passing fare
I no longer think that you are blind
I no longer believe that someday you won't be mine.
This I say with utmost conviction
Because that night, I felt your affection and adoration.
It was as tangible as the sun that shines.
As omnipresent like the air we breathe.
No longer was it merely in words;
I was touched by it, then mauled, and caressed.

But, as I said, in morbidity I thrive.
My strength comes from my bitterness.
If I am writing this, then I am harbouring some resentment.
The only change after that night,
I used to celebrate my bitterness, now I want to rid myself of it.

And that is when I get ensnared by the one true absolute—my aloneness.

Chronicle of Breaking the Chastity of Falling in Love

A course we set on, a collision was imminent.
Celestial celebrations, a supernova and its remnants
A moment so magnanimous, bliss became the revenant
Kill me, tear me, shred me... This ripple in time will always be permanent.

Take me on my path of despair
Riddle it more with the devil's glare
Rid it of any of those angel's stare
Make me walk through all those unholy fairs
But, if it brings me back to this same shore
I'd walk the path, even if it was a million times more unfair.

The contours on your face
Made my febrile heartbeat win a race
Through your hands, I felt my soul
In all these years, I was never this whole
Then when we rung against each other
Giving that words is an abomination, a memory which I will not smother.

The ability to speak, I do not boast.

The gift to think is all I host
Till that night, I was just a ghost
you ushered in a light, making me adore life
the most.

The Alley

And I look out the window
In search of her face,
I long to get a glance
Kept as an art of that blazing maze.
Yes, there was hurting,
No doubt there was pain.
I walked down the alley, which had seen no rain,
I didn't understand, hence I didn't remain!

Not a lion, not a wolf, nor a rat on any day,
He was a human, maybe that's why he had no say.
His thoughts though were of a different ray,
His hair was black, why didn't they turn grey?
As he walked down the alley with immense pain,
He couldn't replace what he could not gain.

She sat down beside them with no expression on her face,
She lay right beside him with nowhere to gaze.
She could've died at this moment, no one would know her name,

But if she lived a while longer, then she would
forget her own name.
As she walked down the alley with shackles
and chain,
She sat down and wondered, who was truly
insane?

Who was the real loser? Was it she, him or
they?
Smothering the light, but it didn't wither
away.
They could be cruel, they could even be pain.

Unfortunately for them, him and her didn't
believe this to be a game.
As the two walked down the alley, amongst
all those slain,
they wondered, what did they gain? Will they
also be slayed?

How ecstatic I would be to tell you about
being happy and gay—
someone who only feels bliss, no sadness on
their face.

Someone who lives in the now with
absolutely nothing to chase.
A person whose values don't originate from
the drains.

But then I ask myself this:
If this man walked down the alley, could he
recognize pain?
Does he know what he'd gain?
Does he know who is insane?
Or,
Will he, like all the others, also walk with
those chains?
In the end, will he also be slayed?

The Pursuit of Unhappiness

Walking on a beach
nowhere pleasant to reach
his life was breached
and on the ocean he did screech

He saw no darkness
He saw no rain
He saw no sorrow
All he saw was pain

He felt no black
He felt no red
He felt no green
He felt no grey

His life was perfect
His life was "perfect"
His life was great
His life was "great"

Happiness was a pressure
Joy was his leisure
Luck was his teaser

Unfortunately, life wasn't his treasure

And as he longed for sadness
He saw an apple of righteousness
Though he was seized by happiness
He was in the pursuit of unhappiness.

The Chronicle of the Half-Moon Day

The Soul

One easily predicts the future, if every day is the same.
This was another day, again elementary at its start.
Its culmination? Right up with the stars.
Control is what it wants me to seek, but I became a tidal wave.
Governed by only the half-moon, maybe that explains my quasi-brave.
Much like the sun, the fission created light.
Though it was in the dead of night, the vision was bright.
Why this obsession with celestial misdirection?
Maybe this is how I say I felt a cosmic connection.

The Mind

The wretched pain of a heartbreak, results in the wicked realisation to be pseudo-fake.
Take drastic steps, make everything into maniacal nets.
Cordon and protect the soul, ensure that there is not one sole.

In this land, we are the king. Always
remember that the king can do anything.
Solitude, initially was your fiend, now is your
closest friend.
I have successfully quarantined, you seem
ready to transcend.
Systems optimised, no hacks, no rupture, no
breaks, no cracks!
Millions of hours of perfection... then came
the onset of that one gesture...
One act resulting in my immense displeasure!

The Observer

Alarms blaring, mind spiralling, frenzy, chaos,
confusion, pandemonium!
Where are the archives? What are the
guidelines?
"Abort! Abort!" screeched every follicle,
"Perimeter breach," screamed every blood
vessel.
Others shrieked, "The mighty wall was to
protect us all..."

The heart emanated a small squeak, the roaring thundering protest was terminated without a brawl.
From now onwards, it becomes the heart's call...

The Heart

Today, I will speak, even if it is for a brief instant.
You reduced me to a mere organ. I am labelled as a burden.
But riddle me this:
When I am at the helm,
You teleport to a different realm.
The mind's mantra: Caution, Precaution, Vacation, and finally, Distortion...
But my Emotion, Commotion, Devotion only lead to self-elevation.
Each memory that I create is permanent.
Each feeling that I generate is pertinent.
I am fragile, but I do not bask in decadence.
Your cowardice, your pessimism, your phobias result not from following me.
Rather, I gift you empathy, humility, compassion and redemption.

Now I command you to retell those events
without convolutions and exclusions.
Document what you felt—no big words, no
complex riddles, no being overtly knightly.
Maybe then, my wrath on this enforced exile
might deter, albeit slightly.

The Mind

Enough of this hoodwinking!
When you shattered, he was left in tatters.
I picked him up, I fixed you.
Still you beat your ideological drum.
Learn practicality! Learn pragmatism!
Vulnerability leads only to becoming a bum.

The Heart

Were you this "wise" when I broke before?
The knowledge that you acquired was because
of that fervour.
Prove me wrong, I shall concede.
But until then, let his words bleed...

The Being

I am not as eloquent as the rest who spoke,

All I realised was that yesterday, I finally
awoke.
Time seemed abstract, yet life felt absolute.
Who knew the one I vehemently ignored,
would leave me absolutely floored?
Logic took a nosedive, instincts came to the
fore,
The current, the proximity, the sharing of
spaces made me shiver to my core.
I can go on, but I have spent all my chips...
As my parting note, I will take the analogy of
ships—
Two separate crafts, traversing on two
individual voyages, rested on the same shore;
When the moment came, they went back to
charter their course.
Maybe they know where they are going,
maybe they don't.
Will they intertwine? Will they become a
fleet?
Will they crash? Will they become obsolete?
What right do I have to predict the future? I
must only thoroughly enjoy the present.
Instead of ruing the fact that we separated,
celebrate the fact that we briefly united.

BEING DUMB

I wanted to break free of the limbo I was in
She wanted to disappear from the land she was in
I stopped believing in new beginnings
She stopped believing in anything ending

Of course, I and she will fall in love
But, before we did, I had a different *she*
And she had a different *he*
He was with her when she was cold
He was with her from times of old
The life of his was vined around her whole
These vines encapsulated her soul
Cut this weed she tried, but kill its root she never could!
Gathering strength seemed improbable, to god's no surprise, she decided to compromise....
Rewarded, she was; her actions bore immediate fruit, she was the queen of a land where the sun would never rise.

I's she was of a different kind
Both their lives were the other's smiles...
Their love was pure, none could make it vile

I's she was very blind, on I's mind, 'she is mine'
He was aware, and she did know
Their heartbeats synced, their souls were one

But fate had different plans, it was determined that this ship sank
Storms came; they stood tall, after each storm they were still strong
It was one year since their inception day, enough is enough—fate wanted to make them pay
A leaf out of a Shakespearean play, celebrations turned into despair
And, unlike all the previous times, the mighty ship could not be repaired!

Protagonist of such a rotten play, his soul now floated on that little plank
In a sudden daze, he entered his limbo phase!
It was unrelenting on both—I and she
My day was no different than night
I could be a glutton, I could be starving, no difference

I could be in the spotlight, I could lurk in the shadows, it still made no difference
Irrespective of what I did, I would be in a place where I hated to be
I knew that my soul was still stuck in limbo
She slowly learned the art of masochism
The keys to the chains were in front of her, but the guilt of being happy seeped into her veins
She wallowed in this darkness which she began calling her home
Two lives in their states of inertia:
One knew that his life can't make any difference to the grand scheme of things,
The other knew that her life isn't one where she would be living for herself.
And, in years and years, he found a land! The land where its queen would only get engulfed into the sand.

How clichéd it is, but every love story is...
No, there were no droopy eyes, no love at first sight
They didn't even feel the air of change
They saw each other, they liked each other

But, both were sure that they would always be
in their eminent cages.
Fate again reared its unnecessary head,
As soon as they accepted their plight, it
decided to change their paths
It was manipulative, it was sinister, it was
kind, but again, it was unforgiving.
I and she had sketched the boundaries, the
universe quashed it in a sudden breeze
And when they got close, he found a place
that he did not dislike
he fell in love with this place from its first
embrace!

This place was in her arms!
He was no longer floating, he found his home!
She was also entrapped in his charm, and felt
happiness and love
Just like him, her inertia also broke, she
wanted to live her own life
And just like that, he broke his limbo, she too
broke her shackles.
Yes, they fell in love!
Not what you find in modern times
The love they share is a special one

Different in minds, but all they want to be is
one
They, like you, want a happy ending
But their scars and wounds are still fresh
Their actions are still weary of those that they
don't cherish
I's she is no longer that *she*, she has made I her
new *he*
Yet, they are scared because of them
Let us just pray they rise from this realm
Because now, nothing can destroy them other
than them being dumb.

Unfaltering Companion

To Pain,

Over a lifetime you've made your presence so impermeable that you could be engulfing me but I still won't allow myself to realise of your existence.

Today I'm asked to invoke your thoughts, connive you to talk to me. I'm sceptical if asked for your to speak incessantly, it will be a forthcoming of the next pandora's box. So, to curb a modern day purana from transpiring, I will ask thee three questions, hoping your response will be limited to just this.

1. Pain, you are nothing but the weapon to enforce karmic justice, would you exist without karma?
2. Heaven is supposed to be the land where you cease to exist or it is the realm which is abundant with your absence. The fallacy still reigns, the only way to be in heaven is to be dead. So, do you cease when I cease, or much like energy you can only be transferred never removed?

3. Pain, when do you feel pain?

I hope pithiness will be your strong suite.

Truly aggrieved by the lack of your remorse (I'm hoping this is a compliment of the utmost honour).

In your captivity till death does us apart.

Your Being.

———————

To my beloved,

Buddy, we are more intertwined than you would know. Just because you can numb yourself doesn't mean you aren't feeling me. You think you are tolerating me? It is me who is putting up with you.

Think of how sensitive you were when you first came into the world, a brush of the wind on your nose, and you started to howl incessantly. Today you stand among the darkest clouds and not bat an eye. Who should be credited for that? Your resolve? Are you that vain?

Also, I'm Pain, so my response should also cause pain. Must be true to my demeanour. I lose my edge for the tiniest of minutes, and suddenly I cease to exist. You forget of my existence for the minutest of instance, and you'll be engulfed in flames. You know this quite well, accept it, "you are existing only to feel pain". A proof "all love ends in grief".

How innocent of you to believe that I can be wielded. All stories are created only to justify my existence. I'm that pepper of life which makes it worthwhile, the new world's version of god and everything else are just the illusion of milk that makes it easier to digest me. But know this, I'm the only absolute. To this you must say cheers.

This brings an end to my retort. I have answered all your questions, maybe in order, maybe not. It's for you to decipher.

Here's to experiencing more of me.

Your unfaltering companion.

Sincerely
Pain

Is there anybody out there?

Hey, you! Yes, you!
Why? Why? Why?
You there! Yes, you!
Why? Why? Why?
You there! Listen here!
You there! Look here!
Why'd you cry when you had to smile?
Yet, you laughed when you had to laugh!
Why'd you starve when you saw the food?
Yet, you ate the same rotten food!
Why'd you jump when you wanted to walk?
Yet, you ran, when you had to run!
Why'd you have to go with them?
Yet, you went all alone!
Why'd you listen to your heart and soul?
When you did exactly what your wicked mind told!
Why'd you wear the colour blue?
Why'd you do the hickety-hoo?
Why'd you nail your sparkling nail?

Why say fine, when you had a fine?
Why'd you commit so many crimes?

Why'd you make so many rhymes?
Hey, you! Yes, you!
Why? Why? Why?

I will not tell you all the why's!
Yet, I will tell you some...
Three of them were asked to me,
Three of them, I shall tell you... then none!
Rhyming is an art of mine,
Symmetry is so much fun.
I live on the brink, with lots of pungent rum!
Hence, I make those crazy puns.
That's the answer to your last.
Now, to answer your second one—
Starving is a mental state, food is nothing but mud.
I live with only my rage, hence I consumed that edible dirt.
That should answer most of them, but I did say I'd give you three retorts.
So, here is my third, satisfy yourself after this, you glorified dirt!

I called you that, because I could no longer rhyme

I have to answer, with a serious mind!
At times you are at nature's will,
There's no point in doing what you want!
But doing something you cannot escape...
So you might as well listen to your wicked mind,
-than to act on others' will.
That is it! There is your three.
Now go, or stay, or be right there!
I'll be lost, because I don't care...
but here are my parting words, your little bonus for this fair,
Never cry when you want to smile, do you want to die that easily?

Hey, you! Come back here!
Don't leave me in this limbo stage!
Hey! Hey, you! Do not go so gently so soon!
Rid me of this perplexity you bestowed!

Hey!
Hey!
Hey!!!!!
Is there anybody out there?

Beaching around

The Beach, its water, sand and sea
Innumerable times seen, encapsulated not always with glee
sparks curiosity, evokes emotions, deduces analogies, draws comparisons,
tonight though, it is all about its clockwork motion, seeming to be my eperisone.
maybe just a culmination of constantly being its denizen?

My first introduction, still a vivid recollection.
Befriending is not what I know, becoming a contravene I knew too well.
But the beach, maybe it could not tell.
It started to play and then we started to play.
Once this bond materialised, the beach became a young boy's living thing
we became my friends, with nothing for either of us to cling
The only one who has stayed true

Anytime, anywhere, any season, always ready,
in spite of generally looking blue!
One of the absolutes from all my days

The beach is only the one who I played with,
and it played back with me always.

With continued interweaves and escapades.
A folly I harboured when ignorance was my
utmost plight
"The beach knows not its powers or its might"
Then my fallacy ceased, when the tsunami
prevailed.
pon looking on it ona bright night with
delight
It was clear, the beach never wants to be the
first to fight!
It roughouses, it gently caresses!
It leaves indelible marks, it gets dusted off!
It inspires, it is pious
Simplicity in its veins, magnanimous in its
reign
Without a roof, yet shelters hoofs to poofs.
Who knew something with so much
versatility, can be so absolute.

The beach can be a lot of things, but being a
variable it would never salute.
It can engulf it all, and ensure that nothing

can be restored
Yet, it chooses just to kiss the floor.
And since then, I have attempted to hold a
diploma in replicating my absolute friend's
persona!

While traversing through the forward linear
motion of the passing time.
Another realisation, and this was when my
youth was in its prime!
At an age when monotony was carcinogenic
to the spirit,
My friend enlightened me, in monotony will
you slay it!
The beach does the same for eternities and
then some more,
Who am I to find remorse in the few decades
where nothing new has come to the fore?

Enough with pondering the yore,
I am quietly placed in thus rather comfortable
place in my lore
The thought enveloping my mind, now even
this page must bore
Does the water that gushes on to the sand,

ever reach the sea's core?
Does the water from the deepest trenches
ever reach the beach's shore?
The curiosity will not stop.
Does it want to?
Does it not?
If I ever get a response, unsatisfactory or not
My follow-ups would be the why, and then
the how and maybe, then can it be bought?

The only thing with my absolute friend,
Though it always plays with me, it never talks
back.
I scream, I whine, I try my best to orate and
convince, but maybe it feels like if it speaks, it
would be called a hack.
Maybe it loves me,
Maybe it despises me,
All I know is thatit greets me the same
everywhere.
Leaving me to my own thoughts,
presumptions, assumptions, and all the likes.

The one quality it shares with all those for
whom I care.

But in the presence of the beach, it often
seems like it's observing me,
Awaiting the inevitable, when will this being
snap!?
Not the one that is accompanied with rage
rather the one where one is forever stuck in
an open cage.

Is this the reason, that tonight I have refused
to jostle?
I have screamed and shouted, hoping for a
response, but it was similar to asking for logic
from an apostle.
I might consider the beach my friend, but
maybe all that I am for the beach is a fossil?
'tis my turn to observe, much like a
domesticated pet
Hoping to be acknowledged, even if it is just
my silhouette.
And to continue pausing with the solitude
laterally
Doing the only thing that comes to me
naturally,
Something innocent that has seldom led to
regret and hopefully never to repent.

I shall also contemplate, and document!

Ha! What is this! I ponder no more
Is this a show of endearment?
Is this a show of its magnificence?
Its wonderful benevolence?
miles of sand, water till the horizon,
but suddenly, only on me there is the lightest of drizzles,
suddenly my spirit is reinvigorated with renewed sizzle.

Skepticism still at the helm, a quality which I will always let overwhelm
Is it to cheer me?
Is it to tease me?
I will never know, nor will it ever tell.
All I hope is that it's not saying, "Friend you and I, we are not so different".
I am still very corruptible, and that does not make me suitable.
The beach you have to be unequivocal, in that you are beautiful, that is indisputable.

I say the next from a selfish place, your beauty

evokes my most cherished pseudo-skill, this
fact is irrefutable.
Your silence is frustrating, but at least I had a
platform to express what otherwise others
would consider inexcusable.
The skeptic in me was overpowered for a
change,
I felt endeared, assured, certain it was not to
derange
I could have been smashed to smithereens by
the wave, splashed incessantly by the rain
but this light drizzle, nothing short of a
gentle embrace, a loving hug.
This light drizzle gave me the feeling of
warmth which I have craved for countless
hours, days and years.
gratitude I have not lost yet, thank you my
absolute, thank you for the acknowledgment.

An observer might say
His own species has discarded him, why
shouldn't the sea? what is the point of
showing him any empathy?"
That observer is me.

Another observer might say
“'tis but a coincidence, not even a happy accident.”
That observer is also me.
But I tell both of them
If people can ardently harbour illusions of speaking to powerful beings, being the vessels to greater beings, and even being the greater beings supplement.
From today I will live with this delusion that the beach was trying to compliment.
And in its compliments, it said, "I understand you, my friend".

All the critters have finally come out without fear
believing no humans to be near
'tis is why I am not coming to you today.
But please know, you are the reason for my elation and bliss.

What an experience, as I pack up to take your leave.
Like the wind I will go away from you,
journeying from one epicentre to the next.

Eventually returning to my absolute friends
Abode again I will recharge myself to go
about.
All my inhibitions about you, my friend, have
slipped away.

Irony seldom leaves my side.
This accomplice of mine ensured that it
reminded me of its presence,
As I was collecting my thoughts to say
goodbye,
Ensuring not to disturb the critters nearby
I was startled by a wanderer who had nothing
to do with me, but came and said hi.

After Your Death

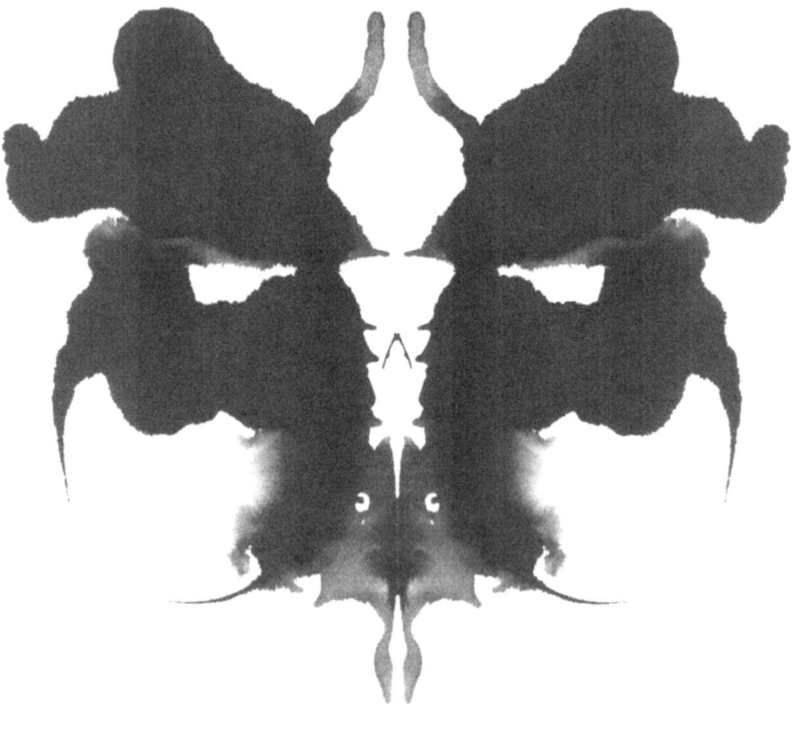

Where once was light, Darkness prevails
Where once was love, wrath resides
Did I say goodbye? At least I couldn't say, "I didn't try!"

The tears I've cried, all fall in vein
with all your lies, the hurt, the blame!
But I still weep, weep at the thought of all of you being this lame...

No loyal friend was ever there
Now, the gall for all of you to say goodbye
In all this you say "I didn't try..."

These tears you cry, come far too late
Take back, take back the lies, the hurt, the blame!
The tears you cry, come far too late...

Save these tears, for when you have to journey in your boat
You will be lost, you will not know home
Use the tears then to steer your route.
But, I know the way, the way to the boat
I know where I will take my next breath
Do you know what you will do after your death?

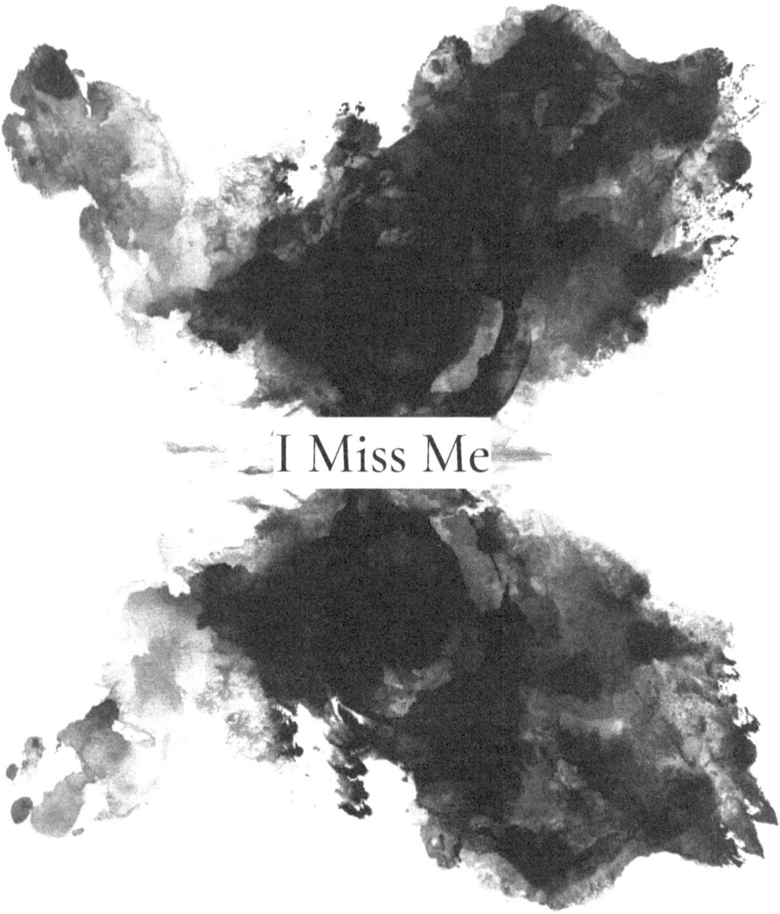

I Miss Me

Where are you now?
The hero from my fantasies
The shadow of the righteous
The reason for all things happy
The one who was crowned the king

Where are you now?
The detective who solved all things gory
The light of all my stories
The one who summoned glory
We had celebrations and carnivals in this purgatory
Someone I should've been, but I mistook you for an allegory
Please forgive me, I am on my knees apologising.
Believe me when I say that I am sorry!

I left my aspirations
you were my inspiration
I left it for unworthy admonitions
And on this night, I wish I was you... I wish I really was you!
(I Miss ME)

Come back now, I already said sorry
In my sleep, I dream about you, these nights
it's only about you.

Stuck in this darkness, which is creeping and
hunting me down
I peered and saw these vicious serpents hatch
Engulfing all things in this town
Something I am expected to match
I wish I could say I never did, but I wish I
never did

I performed my own treason
Castrated and mutilated you without reason
Just come back tonight
Won't you come back tonight?

I change my mind, I want you to return as the
voice inside my head (I Miss ME)
Please just return, I swear I won't let you go
out of my sight (I Miss ME)
If you come back, I know for sure that we
won't wither and die (I Miss ME)
Reappear and see me nurse you back to
health (I Miss ME)

Let's not waste time, don't be shy, I know of
my follies (I Miss ME)

I change my mind, I want you to return as the
voice inside my head (I Miss ME)
Please just return, I swear I won't let you go
out of my sight (I Miss ME)
If you come back, I know for sure that we
won't wither and die (I Miss ME)
Reappear and see me nurse you back to
health (I Miss ME)
Let's not waste time, don't be shy, I know of
my follies (I Miss ME)

I change my mind, I want you to return as the
voice inside my head (I Miss ME)
Please just return, I swear I won't let you go
out of my sight (I Miss ME)

If you come back, I know for sure that we
won't wither and die (I Miss ME)
Reappear and see me nurse you back to
health (I Miss ME)
Let's not waste time, don't be shy, I know of
my follies (I Miss ME)

I change my mind, I want you to return as the
voice inside my head (I miss me)
I change my mind, I want you to return as the
voice inside my head (I miss me)
I change my mind, I want you to return as the
voice inside my head (I miss me)

You aren't coming back, are you?
I have ripped you off existence itself

I miss me....

Finding Meaning

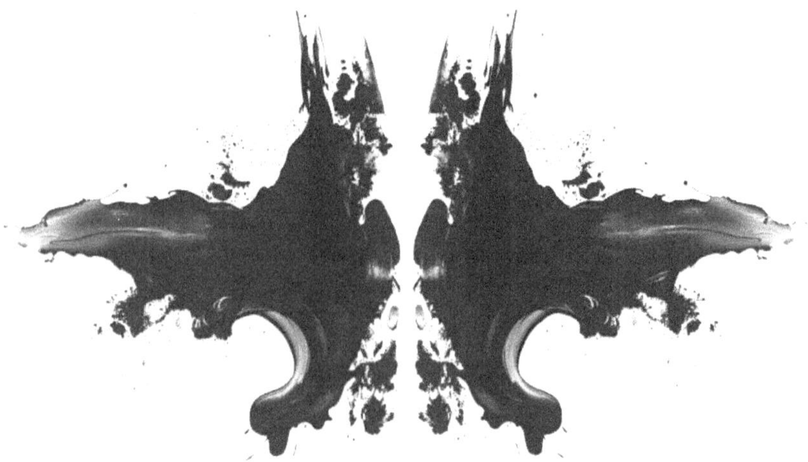

The burning sun on a bright day
The blue sky again on a bright day
The dead night after a bright day
The bread in my hand is a blazing glaze

Words when combined mean nothing
Words when combined can mean something
Death and life, are they the same?
Can death not be the end of a game?

The sun and sky could mean nothing
The sun and sky could mean everything
The bright day comes after a night dead
The dead night comes at life's end

The inferences made
The differences laid
The madness swayed
The Randomness, The Randomness, The Randomness

If truth be told
The day is bright, because it can
The night is dead, because it can
Words mean, because it can

death comes, because it can
If a sun burns, then it just burns
if a sky is blue, then it is just blue
If a life is conceived, then only a life is
conceived

Why do you, my heroes of Plato, need to find
meaning in all?

Cutting the Monkey's Tail

Losing sight, what a fright.
Losing height, the water has dried.
Dawning of night, rebirth of a knight.
Men and women! Do not fight.
Kings and Queens! Where is your might?

Kneel, bow, cut his hands!
Scream, shout, fuse the band.
Gorge his eyes, flog his skin.
Rip his heart, reroute his brain
In this age, the might of the mighty is
measured by his gonads.

Where art thou, my love?
Loving my neighbour, me amor...
Unfortunately, it wasn't figuratively.
Let me rape the victim's mind once more.

How do we build a scale?
Why are we condemned to fail?
The little nanny is so pale...
And finally, who cut the monkey's tail?

To Alcoholism

Sleep comes to everyone
Sleep comes to a tired one
Sleep happens to anyone
Yet dream you have, when sleep is none.

The dream you had, you didn't care
The dawn to come, didn't you stare?
Gazing upon the long dark knight, appeared a wild tear
And with that one, came a herd of violent fear!

Where is my weed, I sow the seed.
Where is my steed, I sow the seed.
When should I read? I sow the seed.
Wait, a good deed! I sow the seed.
I sow the seed, I got its fun.
I sow the seed, I saw it run.

Go! There's your weed, on your steed
Alas, I shall read the property deed
I sow the seed, not for a mouth to feed

I sow the seed for a dream I had seen
The dream was of Complexity One!

The transition turn... no! No gun!!
Pure it was, like the life of a sun
It was fun... No! No Pun!!
All I did was ingest the rum...

Rhyme to Confuse

Have you ever thought of me?
Me as in me, not me. "Me"?
Got the rhyme? Oh! You couldn't see...
A then B, you guessed it, then comes C!

How random does it seem?
That madam, she orders the team!
What! The lion's drinking herbal tea..
Did the Titanic really embark on that sea?
We know how knowledgeable you could be!
Now make yourself busy, more than a worker bee...
Did you pay the young man's fees?
Why did you play with my friend's car keys?

Hope you aren't as confused as me.
Structure comes with a capital T,
Like how A comes after B and C.
Just how she meant everything to be!

Tamed to his Thought

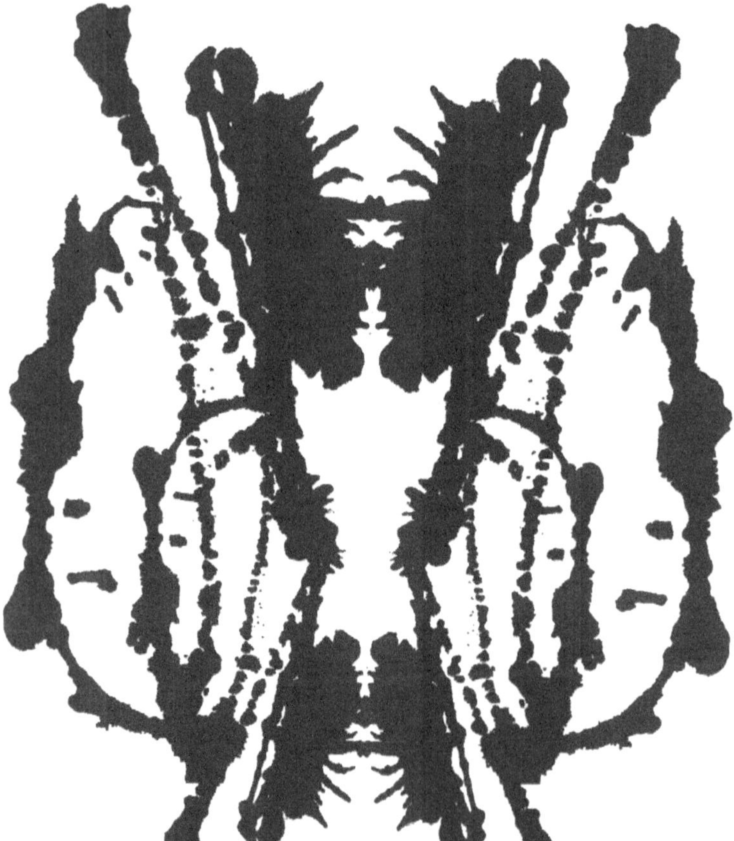

A new end or an old start—
this is what the righteous king thought
on the eve of his mighty conquest
while sitting at his lustrous banquet.

The king had not just one name
his fame was an ode to his game
if challenged, never could he be tamed
He put everyone else to shame.

Yet, the king had not come of age
though victorious, he was not a sage
he thought the world to be "his stage"
unaware of all its hidden rage.

Tomorrow he would set ablaze
unlock the future and its maze
give the world some to chase
over the top, he wanted to gaze.

So, while sitting at his lustrous banquet
on the eve of his mighty conquest
the king was still a victim to his thought
a new end, or an old start.

Origin of Colours

In my darkness, I see black!
Oh, really? I thought I saw pink.
When I bleed, I bleed red.
Astounding, my brother! I bleed yellow...
In my pain, I become blue.
Applause galore! Common facts, you know too well.
In my sadness, I am surrounded by grey.
Congratulations, at least you don't feel green.
In my celebrations, I use orange.
I honestly believed you'd use white.

ENOUGH! Do not utter another word!
I spake as a reaction to the opening of your gong-spewer.
I now sense a rant coming my way!

Destroyed I've been many a times,
Reason not always akin to mine.
Passions I have, not leading to unsavoury crimes,

Still the order was passed to murder me in my prime!
Forsaken I was, so I forsake all.

An honest attempt to be essential in every sphere,
But, somehow the same algorithm followed:
Started to enjoy, locked in a cell.
Locked in a cell, I worked my way out.
Once out, shoved to the corner.
Shoved to the corner, I worked my way out.
Again, once out, back into the cell.
Again out, back to the corner.
To end this cycle, I jumped into this well.
Dismay follows a little too close! I was deemed unfit to drown, too.
I made peace with myself, accepted my fate,
Though I believed myself to be unfit to be given this fate.
But, greater powers wished for it, so I became this.
Now you come, dancing and prancing, raining on my cage.
Leave me be, let me be!
There are millions of other brothers who yearn to be bothered.
Let me speak the colours that I see.
Let me be in the colours that I feel.
Begone! Begone! Begone!

Melodrama coupled with melancholy,
I thought I'd give you company but you love
your monotony.
A monologue to justify your solitary.
So I am going, all set to leave,
But as a parting gift I leave you this:
The sky is the origin of all the colours that we
see.

The Plight of Mountains

The plight of mountains
The flight of clouds
The right of trees
The fright of rivers
All the amalgamation of chance
The *how* determined
The *why* a mystery
Two hundred thousand years have passed
Yet no closer to knowing the *why* than from
its first sight

As a child, I knew that I didn't know
In not knowing, I knew more
When I was a king, I knew that I knew
But in my knowing, I knew nothing

Circles in the faith of fruits
Triangles in the faith of smoke
Skin in the faith of uncertainty
Crosses in the faith of restraint
Five-pointed stars in the faith of damnation

Only two don't exist in nature
A chronic battle to be loved and not wanted
A losing fight to be wanted but not needed

A tyrannous right to be accepted and righteous
An ominous scar of failing all

A need to be affiliated
Entwined with the want to be secluded
A want to be loving
Estranged when you need to be loved
Altruism is nothing but making selfishness complicated
Failure is when I am adjudicated?

Melancholy is accompanied by dismay
Grief with despair
Helplessness with haplessness
Ironically, solitude also has the company of silence
But I am companioned only by myself

Knowing doesn't negate the longing
Longing for affection

Longing for partnership
Longing for appreciation
Longing for applause

Longing for acceptance
Longing to belong
Success defined by the achievement of all?

I am at my best when left to my behest.
The embodiment of the conundrum in failure
is success.
The paradox of not achieving nothing if I
decide to move.
The very facet of existing to only eventually
being removed.
Now I know the plight of this mountain.

When Clouds Descend

An ease when we stroll through green
A weariness when we are engulfed in black
Relaxed when basking in blue
But, an innocuous feeling persists when
walking through white

Its abode in the sky
Its existence well determined
Multitude of purposes
Its death is our life

Flying like any ordinary man
Blowing in the wind
Seen all the secrets of the world
Holding treasures bequeathed to none

So abundant, yet cannot be captured
So vast, yet cannot be ascended
Always visible, always elusive
Never fallible, never palpable

Its fury when it bursts
Its thunderous roars when they collide
Sending shockwaves as reminders
Even a lunatic must succumb to its dark side

But when it does grace us
We cannot blast it out of existence
We cannot cut it to make it insignificant
We cannot shoot it down
We can not punch it away
We can only be engulfed in it
We can only hope, ideally with patience, that
it decides to pass through us.

Causations?

Correlations?

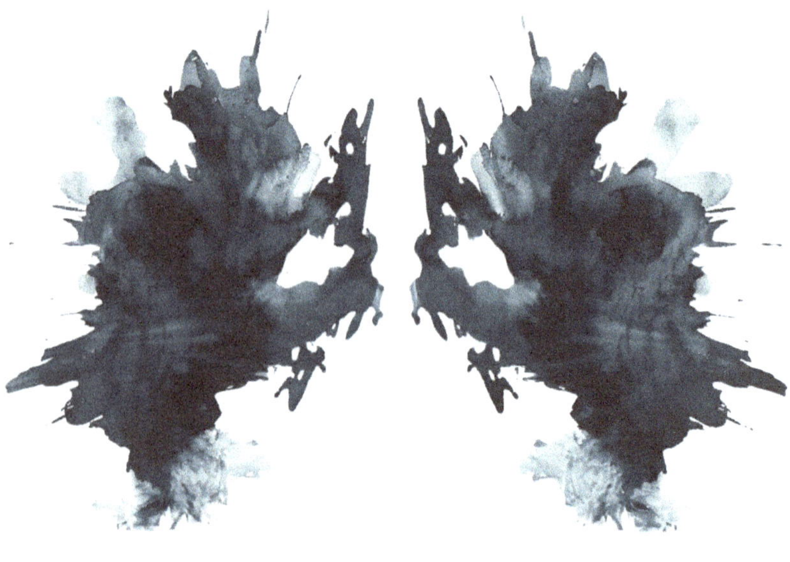

For a small nozzle, the air pressure was lost.
For the air pressure, the tire was lost.
For the tire, the car was lost
For the car, the message was lost.
The message didn't arrive, the love was lost.

Happiness should justify existence itself.
Existence occurs when pain is cultivated.
Pain is the result of eternal suffering.
In suffering then, there is thriving.

Loud noises hiding your real disdain
Camouflaging your eyes who are fighting to explain
Are you seeking an asylum?
Are you looking for a sanctuary?

Commute longer than time spent in the destination.
This makes the journey the destination.

Incessantly on the move, ironically never moving.
Irony is always lost, not because it can't be found. Ironic.

In the pauses and stillness,
The enchantress is withholding the elixir.
Enjoy the wait, and be rewarded,
With the true meaning of reaching the destination.

A belief from not within caused a spark that transformed into a greatest flame.
My god has intertwined and interwoven with the universe and with time.
They are in a place where the past, present, and future coincide.
But in my land of objective delusion, I attempt to be a protagonist with subjective affiliation.

Did the god try before to awaken this flame?
Did the same god try to douse the spark which was paper-thin?

Was the belief a part of the relief? Or will it be grief leaving me once again in disbelief?
I comprehend very well that my thoughts and words are not a part of my genetic code.

A boon or bane, I still know not.
Am I a medium? Was the belief the medium?
Just one certainty, I am a culmination of
things because of a result of causations and
not correlations.

New Eden

A start I must with the greatest line
A belief I held for the greatest time
Between an actor and villain, chose the mime
A prayer, "both death along with life isn't mine!"
An amalgamation of constant pressure
Constant stagnation of finding treasure
Not for mine, rather for others pleasure
An achievement that has no measure.
Expose not your bare skin,
Showcase not your one true sin
Learn not how to win
Never pin your failures to the chin.
To think is to become
To become is to be
To be is to flow
To flow is not acceptable to me.
Principal of principles
Be fine to pay your fine
No wine do not whine
no tail? tell a tale!
Sense is not about letting go
Sense is not about screaming after stubbing your toe

Sense is not to cry to your foe
Sense is not to continue to woe.
In stoicism, there is true meaning
In bliss, you are not gleaning
In misery, you are not feigning
All experiences are only to document,
Your emotions need management.

Here is the crux:
Our yardstick is not derived from animals
Our purpose is to better our ancestors
Our minds, free from rudimentary and
convoluted aspects of just good and evil
Our souls will always be restricted to
purgatory and its ills
Better we must, through emotional
attenuation
Better we must, through feeling no attrition
Unravel the core, unlock the pore
Make yourself a knowledge whore!
Your journey to the large nothingness
Will be wrought with spaces of emptiness
But when you reach the unquenchable
darkness
Do the above, or else you will be—

Responsible for accentuating the illness
The evolution of weakness
The celebration of madness
Journeying joyfully to dampness
Hearing sounds of only unholiness
Witnessing wholeheartedly the blindness
Reminiscing the shrewdness
Creating all but homesickness
Realising truly, the lack of consciousness.
My friend, 'tis not too late
Don't wait for a further date
Please don't condemn yourself to dumb fate
In you, there lies the ability to be great
All you must do is not tempt hate,
Don't become its bait!
Why do you wait?
Follow not blindfolded to this estate
"god" will test your ability to sedate, berate,
frustrate, conjugate
If you pass or fail in this innate test to dilate
I am here to take you through this gate.
To Eden or to hades is upon your ability to
debate.

Entourage

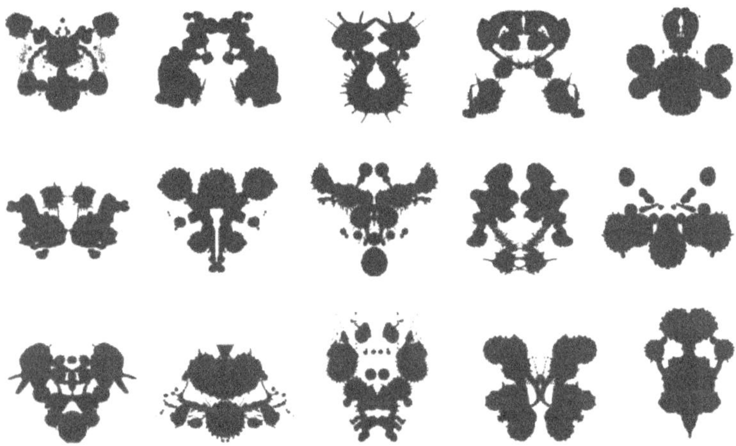

Reflection

A thick asylum of clouds has engulfed the sky.
The rays of the sun have decided to not even try to break this barrage.
On this day of tyrannous comfort, the heart wants to be able to fly.
Why have a barrier? Why this distance? Let me become a part of your entourage!

Realism

There's a drizzle, wind its companion.
It seems like they were sent from the garden of night coral jasmine...
Ah! So beautiful, and yet so painful. Finally, I have broken my mirage.
Why have a barrier? Why this distance? Let me become a part of your entourage!

Redundancy

Why have a barrier? Why this distance? Let me become a part of your entourage!

Why have a barrier? Why this distance? Let me become a part of your entourage!

Why have a barrier? Why this distance? Let
me become a part of your entourage!
Why have a barrier? Why this distance? Let
me become a part of your entourage!

Recluse

There's my phonebook, there's my telephone,
do I have someone to call?
There's my house door, there's the doorbell,
do I need to enthral?
Let me fetch my silverware stored in my
wareroom, I shall pour all of the alcohol.
Such a pleasure that is bought with this
surety, not one do I have to appal.

Recalcitrant

Disobeying an authority is all but child's play.
Mutiny to another being makes at least one
person gay.
Ungovernable, intractable, unmanageable,
insubordination—

Performing these actions to an outside force
makes you a rebel.

I have gone one step further: I oppose my instincts to survive.
Appeasement is the truest form of disobedience.
Now, let me be a part of your entourage.

Remorse

So much talent, so much potential.
In all humility, I know I used to have so much ability.
I could mesmerise, I could humanise... I could fall in love.
Instead, all I did was punch my guts with my own boxing glove.
Your troupe needs a circus dove. Let me be a part of your entourage!

Repulsion

Oh look, my reflection! Ugh, I feel nausea! Is it my appearance, or my incoherence?
Such ugliness, coupled with antipathy, but still a focus on apathy...

My disgust, detestation, repugnance, revulsion comes from my sabotage.

Why have a barrier? Why this distance? Let me become a part of your entourage!

Realisation

Waiting for the invite,
To rid my hunger, it is I who has to bite.
When I look back, it is I who creates my own montage.
No more barriers, no more distance, here is one more for your entourage!

Rest

The fleeting clouds look like they have come to a standstill.
My thoughts have materialised into one.
Come now, hopefully with a smile, it is time for me to camouflage.
Let us unite, you are my light, I shall now accept me in my own entourage.

The Ballad of a Bard

Beethoven, Bach, Mozart
Voltaire, Schopenhauer, Tolstoy
Akbar, Alexander, Ashoka
Jesus, Buddha, Muhammed
Footprints in time? They have earmarked time
Where is this innovation?
Why hasn't there been a new god?
These people... were they all just frauds?
Reign over us, oh great lord!
you spoilt us with your insidious lard
Only consolation... we have this bard!
Come now Bard, tell us our story...
Even if you're hard... don't leave us this scarred.

I wake, like the thousand nights before
The sun still shines like seven nights ago
Why don't you have quality, you ask?
Where is your messiah, you question?
Are you robbed of worshipping your contemporaries?
Must you satisfy this need by praising unseen entities?

Are you stagnating, Are you the inconsequence?
Is your existence loquacious?
Are you longing to be pugnacious?

Bard! Halt Now!
You are an iconoclast, don't invigorate it by infusing hedonism
Tell us in a plain and simple tongue,
Who do we follow?
Who is our hero?
Who is the spirit of our sun?

You insult the Bard, but the Bard is not a king
You call me agnostic, but the Bard knows he is not royal
You tell the Bard that he is superfluous, but the Bard knows that he lacks scholarly skill
The Bard is a bard; all he knows is to sing.
When you perish, this will be the song of yore...
Humans crucified humans,
He brought machines to the fore
Insecurities of his father
Made his loins sore

Dearth of innovation
Made them all a bore
Access to unbound knowledge
Yet, they performed these mediocre chores.
Your songs will not be of glee and dance
Your songs will make all your ancestors
mourn
You are the generation of trivial pursuit
You are the result of intellectual incest

Ha! Bard! Enough of your madness
Say something true, don't make us this
restless

Brother, look! This clown will do what we say
All he wants is cash in exchange

Bard go away, we have found our documenter
He will be a much, MUCH better soothsayer!

Solitary Storyteller

Droplets when they fall from the dark clouds
Herald the imminent arrival of lighting and
thunder
The thoughts that have come from this
storyteller's mind
Will herald the culture in the coming times.
Society has divided men and times into
worshippers and the worshipped
businessmen and the soldier
leaders and the followers
Revered and the degenerates
but the storyteller remains the one constant
throughout them all.
His ancestors have routinely
Documented events, obscured the facts—
The news casters with their acts
Celebrated the victors, marred their legacy—
King's courtesans with their need to ascertain
supremacy
Prophesied utopia, delivered dystopia; the
messiah's attempting to mask their dystonia
Enabling an escape, distraction to shackle; the
creatives making all believe they are the
sheep, but actually the jackal.
Their kind knew very well, they only create to

manipulate.
This storyteller, an individualist, an outsider.
Events led him to become a great despiser,
That made him an even better adorer.
Ready to sacrifice himself at a moment's
notice
Not seeking a reason to go beyond the stars,
where the light does not reach
Nor seeking a reason to go into the depths of
the earth, where still the light does not reach!
Oh storyteller, your companion I long to be...
Oh storyteller, won't you talk to me?
Oh storyteller, please tell your story to me...

Oh great flatterer—
You know how to sway my wearied spirit
Banking on my self-imposed exile
But I know you! you are a necrophile!
You! You are the reason for the corruption of
my ancestors.
You position yourself just to be the ears,
After all, what would a magnum opus be, if it
were not to have any stares
You and your kind are the most despicable
type of men

because you can never despise yourself.
You know the inherent need of a storyteller, it is to share,
Share their learning, wisdom, thoughts, creations
You know they need, they need only an audience
But that audience that gathers should not be based on allegiance or obedience
but you companions, who act like the storyteller's guardians
entice crowds with the threats of disobedience.
You get us hooked on applause and ovations
a narcotic drug whose effect is stronger than long-term use of opioids
You continue to respect your skill to galvanise
While you erode our skill to alchemize
Your power increases based on our talent oscillating
Not between the true, genuine and upstanding
Rather between the gallantry, farcicality, and what the spectators consider to be outstanding.

I blame thee not entirely for the storyteller's demise
In a companionship, all fallacy is equally shared,
Because of this intoxication, and to no longer feel this isolation.
The storyteller's curiosity and terror become fatigued.
Poets becoming journalists, novelists became ghostwriters, lacking the will to be intrigued.
My kind has eroded their gift
Trying to abjectly reject the bright blessed loneliness
Not realising, loneliness is a part of this gift!
Without loneliness you inherently intentionally and inevitably destroy the storytelling activeness
Whitewashing, retelling, recreating, rehashing, debilitating, interjecting, insulting.
All to ensure that solitude, seclusion, desolation, sequester cannot exist in their proximity
Now the gifted kind transmorph into becoming just another story hearer,
Not realising that for every thousand of them,

there is just one lone story teller.
So I refuse to have your companionship,
I admonish thee!
Even though you might bring me the
audience
Give me the platform to be a celebration
I will rather be true to my bestowal,
than be swayed and become your renewal.

Oh, Storyteller! Your purpose you did not
fulfil
In these tropical times, it is best to live near
the wild equator.
The mild animals needed something new
If you associated with I, I had the gun
possessed by only a few
If all else would've failed, we could pluck the
donkey's eyes and then make it laugh and go
to sleep.
We could've called all the gods
Then called in the gods
And called on the dogs
This proposition for you to traverse the vast
tropic corridors comes to a halt

Oh, Storyteller! Your purpose you did not fulfil
In these tropical times, it is best to live near the wild equator.
The mild animals need something new.
If you associate with I, I have the gun—possessed by only a few.
If all else would fail, we could pluck the donkey's eyes and make it go to sleep.
We could've called all the dogs,
Then called in the dogs,
And called on the gods.
This proposition for you to traverse the vast tropic corridors comes to a halt.

I go back, back to my bard! At my command, he will even consume water with only salt.

Sermon of the Pious Philosopher

I know now with almost great certainty and conviction, the meaning of life, the reason for existence, why we live and our purpose to be.

The journey to reach this juncture was rather short, but extremely arduous and toiling. Much of the philosophers have already exclaimed it, along with the many souls who have embraced it.

To enunciate upon this journey is rather futile and an attempt to document it will all but be counterproductive. It's rather the destination that is primordial and with this comes the rather anticlimactic nature of my realisation.

The purpose of life is to not have a purpose. The meaning of life is that there is none, the reason for existence is to just exist, and living is only about being able to embrace death. All purpose is self-imposed, and anything self-imposed will ensure we mould our conscious selves to make an attempt to fulfil it.

Its subsequent failure or in the rather off chance of realising it, becomes critical in the donning of the next moment or phase.

This fallacy makes us subservient to our own selves. Would you ever allow a mutiny against yourself?

But living without a purpose brings to the forefront our subconscious selves, which if put in charge inherently has a better understanding of the intricacies that surround us. And this makes living rather interesting.

Now to elaborate on the meaning of life: all of human existence has gone into essentially elaborating the "how's" and still absolutely flummoxed at the "why's" with the most closest reasoning possible lying in its "infinite randomness"—this was just another outcome or a supposed higher power decided so, whose reason for doing so is nothing but "because they can". And in this predominant explanation that is dominant in this timeline, we are looking to find meaning.

Just take the chaos and bask in the randomness.
Giraffes and rhinos exist but not unicorns,
Thus, you facing a certain experience is just that—nothing more profound.

Now let's talk about existence. Our existence matters not to us but to those who we are around. What matters to us is surviving. To survive we all but need air, water, food, and sleep. Anything else is indulgence. Existence, therefore, mutilates into thriving, which indefinitely leads to needing approval and acceptance, and again all our actions then get marred because of the need for recognition—whether for our actions or in most situations, our in-actions.

As soon as we filter out these impurities,
Taking inspiration from all things governed by nature and not from the illusion of free will, then there will be the instant realisation that all things exist just because they must

and for no other reason.

And finally let's elaborate on living. Nothing in the entirety and vastness of this or any other conceivable universe other than the ones we concoct in and through our minds can grant the human body immortality. And this is enough to know wholeheartedly that our entire living is to die. How effortless our death is, depends on how we live, which is complex and convoluted yet always fluid, but only the darkness of death is absolute.

Denying this to reign upon our consciousness is something imprinted into our DNA, because eventually it erodes the very need for us to survive. But not needing to survive is the most fundamental step toward realising true freedom!

Exit, Stage Left!

Smitten by wanderlust
Amongst the stars, convinced I was in my unending forward thrust
Enthralled by the escapades of this lonely city and its unfamiliar committee
No house or home, a life of an unknown.
The only asset I boasted of was the paper with my name and my ink blotch stains
Companionship eluded me, always scorned by love.
Yet, in my heart, its significance never lost, values I'd always try to impart
Dejected routinely, admired rarely
Tranquil hymns of joyous tomorrows reigned on my lips
Scarred on my skin, charred because unwilling to sin,
Peer into my eyes—if you did, you'd still find an authentic smile.
Embrace I did this lonely city, becoming another member of the unknown community
My wanderlust continued to drive me forward
I'd whisper every night, "I am one amongst the stars, I will not be slaughtered."

Credence and faith in the following thought:
"Talent endowed by greater gods, question not why I must be ploughed"
Prudence and wraiths slowly crept into my trade
I experienced a malicious joy when I saw my body and spirit fading away
Time thieving at my empty safe
The treasures so dear to me, made way only to its grave.
Dawned upon me a thought so wild, it shackled my core and beseeched a disgusting bile:
The god who breathed into me these organic qualities was replaced by gods who denounced inborn capabilities.

Soon, in this struggle with stupidity,
I metamorphosed into a brutal man.
Brothels, bottomless bottles
Argument against a stupid brow malformed into a clenched fist
The suffering I wanted to inflict made my suffering only greater.

Art was that which made my stomach growl
So, I started to embrace all that I previously found fowl
I lent my voice, soul and intellect to causes I never believed in
Shoved down my throat corrupt mainsprings, which tasted worse than battery acid mixed with semen
I shattered in entirety the integrity of self
My art and artwork stopped to matter. It was all taken away by that green elf
I started to lose my higher art
I envisioned it to be displayed upon the Great Festival Road of Humanity
Soon, I saw that it was used to lure poor exhausted and sick humans
Its purpose was reduced to intoxication and aiding the madness

Annoyed and fed-up with this excuse of a life
All pleasures I dejected—some out of fear and rigorous strife
Liens with hope broken beyond repair
I no longer had an excuse to crib or complain
Justice, I learned, happened only through

barter
Another injustice I bore in silence, without attaining the status of a martyr.
An explanation, I wanted for my helplessness
This was only met with more dejection and haplessness.

This world....
This world of castles, thrones and crowns
World of society, an enemy to humanity
A world whose tradition dictates to lust for wealth
A world where each body is battered and each soul is thirsty
Vision blurred, hearts wretched and scorned
Delusions of world-mindedness betwixt illusions of sorrow-headedness
A world where the human entity is a mere toy
A world established on graves of dreams, pleasure, and joy
A world where dying is more profitable than living
A world where youth is a curse
A world where the young decorate themselves, only to go upon the shelves

Love also is nothing more than a business ordeal
Being loved and cherished is not viable
Virtues of loyalty and comradery are not to be cherished.

Celebrate it or burn it, I don't care.
Turn it to ashes, you will not need massive matches.
This world is not mine, I no longer want any part of it.
Remove it from my sight, I have perished to its might.

Credits

Front and Back Cover

Artwork and Design- Sumona Mukherjee

Gratitude to the Readers

A simple word,
Used incessantly and abhorrently around the world.
Yet, when I speak of it today,
I say it in its core essence, instead of issuing a communique.

This word is "Thanks!"
And though short, it is generally sweet.
I would fall in my own ranks,
If I didn't take this opportunity to elaborate, instead of being discreet.

I Thank you for the opportunity.
I Thank you for including me in this community.
I Thank you for tolerating my lunacy.
I Thank you for looking past my buffoonery!
I thank you for your support immensely.
I hope this list isn't too mushy.
And though I leave a little gloomily,

I look onward to influencing this world positively.
That is my promise and oath, hopefully to continue this legacy!